cards
for all seasons

Connie Westenberg

FORTE PUBLISHERS

Contents

© 2004 Forte Uitgevers, Utrecht
© 2004 for the translation by the publisher
Original title: *CQ wenskaarten voor alle seizoenen*

All rights reserved. No part of this publication may be copied, stored in an electronic file or made public, in any form or in any way whatsoever, either electronically, mechanically, by photocopying or any other form of recording, without the publisher's prior written permission.

ISBN 90 5877 455 4

This is a publication from
Forte Publishers BV
P.O. Box 1394
3500 BJ Utrecht
The Netherlands

For more information about the creative books available from Forte Uitgevers:
www.forteuitgevers.nl

Final editing: Hanny Vlaar, Hilversum, the Netherlands
Photography: Marc Wouters, Pulle, Belgium
Styling: Connie Westenberg, Echt, the Netherlands
Cover and inner design: BADE creatieve communicatie, Baarn, the Netherlands
Translation: Michael Ford, TextCase, Hilversum, the Netherlands

Preface	3
Techniques	4
Step-by-step	5
Materials	7
It's autumn	8
Spring is in the air	11
Let the sun shine	14
Pets in the Christmas spirit	15
Snowdrops in the snow	18
The height of summer	20
It's Christmas	22
Sparkling candles	26
Playful butterflies	28
Large and small stickers	30
Pictures of stencils	10, 19 and 23
Pictures of punches	27 and 31

Preface

CQ is a technique for making greeting cards which combines six different mosaic punches with matching embossing/embroidery stencils and mosaic stickers. Thanks to the many variations these materials offer, there are countless possibilities for making cards.

I enjoyed writing this book. CQ is suitable for making cards for every season and I have tried to show this with the cards in this book. Crafters will also be able to enjoy punching, embossing and embroidering all year round. The matching mosaic stickers give a surprising and decorative result to a homemade card with which you will surprises many people. After all, who would not wish to receive such a sparkling, embossed card with decorative embroidery?

Connie

Techniques

What is CQ?

CQ is an abbreviation for cum quoque which means equal in Latin. It is a combination of six mosaic punches, six mosaic embossing/embroidery stencils and six mosaic stickers. For every punch, there is a matching stencil which has the same patterns of the same size and there is also a sticker sheet which also has the same patterns. That is why countless combinations are possible.

The difference between paper and card

Thin paper is called paper and thick paper (more than 150 g/m^2) is called card.

You need thin paper when punching, otherwise it is too difficult to punch through the paper or the punch may break. A punch aid is not always necessary, but is useful.

You need thicker paper when embossing, otherwise it may tear. For this reason, we use card for embossing. You can use either card or paper of a different colour to stick a punched strip or a 3D picture on. The material used is, however, just called paper.

All the colours of the cArt-us collection are available both as paper and card.

The Canson Mi-Teintes (160 g/m^2) collection is suitable for both embossing and punching. Depending on the use, it is, therefore, either called paper or card.

Photograph 1: Mosaic punching

Use thin paper when punching (80 - 130 g/m^2). Draw a row of squares or a frame of joined squares (2.2 x 2.2 cm) on the back of the chosen paper. Hold the punch upside down so that you can see the pencil lines and punch the patterns in every other square. Do this carefully, so that the patterns remain inside the pencil lines.

Photograph 2: Embossing

Only use card thicker than 150 g/m^2 when embossing. You can emboss the squares between the punched patterns or you can draw some squares (2.2 x 2.2 cm) on a separate piece of card. Place the stencil on a light box and place the card on top. Use an embossing stylus to carefully push the lighted parts of the stencil. If you wish, use Pergasoft so that the ball of the embossing stylus slides easily over the card. Next, cut out the embossed squares and stick them between the punched mosaic patterns. You can also embroider them first (see Embroidery).

Photograph 3: Pricking

After you have embossed the squares, place them, one by one, on the pricking pattern of the embossing/embroidery stencil which has been placed on a light box. Prick the holes using a fine 1-needle perforating tool. Do not press too hard, otherwise you will

1. Draw squares (2.2 x 2.2 cm) on the back of the paper and punch the patterns alternately.

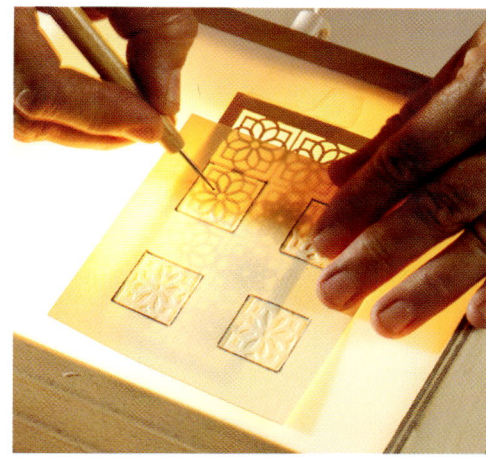

2. Place the card on top of a stencil which lies on a light box and emboss the patterns.

3. Leave the card on the light box and carefully prick the embroidery pattern.

4. Turn the card over and prick the embroidery holes again from the front of the card. Embroider the pattern.

damage the light box. Prick the holes again from the front of the card.

Photograph 4: Embroidery

Use Sulky embroidery thread which is available in many different colours. Stick the start and the end of the thread to the back of the card. Next, cut out the embroidered squares and stick them between the punched mosaic patterns. Another possibility is to draw around the row of squares or the frame and to emboss or embroider the squares alternately.

Mosaic stickers

Stick matching mosaic stickers between the embossed and embroidered squares. Next, cut out the embossed frame or row of squares. You can also use the outer edge and the inlays of the stickers to produce a nice positive-negative effect on the card. Carefully remove the outer edge of the sticker from the sticker sheet using the point of a knife and stick it on card or paper. Next, carefully cut around the edge using a knife. Carefully remove the inlays of the sticker from the sticker sheet using template tape. Stick tape of the correct width on the inlays (rub over the top with a finger nail so that they stick properly to the tape) and stick them on paper or card. Press them down firmly and carefully remove the tape. There are also two large stickers (see last chapter) and some border stickers on the sticker sheets.

3D cutting

Cut out all of the first picture and use glue to stick it on the card. For the second layer, do not cut out what is in the background. The third layer consists of one or a number of parts in the foreground. Use drops of 3D glue to stick the second and third layers on the card.

Materials

- CQ embossing/embroidery stencils: 2859 to 2864
- Mosaic punches: 2859 to 2864
- CQ mosaic stickers: gold or silver 2801 to 2812
- cArt-us card (220 g)
- cArt-us punch paper (120 g)
- Romak separating sheets (130 g)
- Embossing light box
- Embossing stylus
- Pergasoft
- Sulky embroidery thread
- Fine embroidery needle
- Fine Pergamano® 1-needle perforating tool

- 3D cutting sheets: Marianne Design, Picturel, Marjoleine and Block 3D
- Adhesive stones
- Punch aid (if desired)
- 3D glue
- 3D scissors
- Double-sided adhesive tape

- (Photo) glue
- Make Me! template tape
- Non-permanent adhesive tape
- Adhesive tape, pencil
- Cutting mat and cutting knife
- Transparent ruler with a metal cutting edge (Securit)

punch

example of a matching punch, stencil and sticker sheet

stencil

part of a sticker sheet (reduced in size)

It's autumn

What you need
- CQ embossing/embroidery stencils:
  2859, 2860 and 2861
- Mosaic punches: 2859, 2860 and 2861
- Gold CQ mosaic stickers: 2801, 2803, 2805 and 2809
- cArt-us card:
  cream (241), dark green (309) and violet (425)
- cArt-us punch paper: cream (241) and old red (517)
- Canson Mi-Teintes punch paper:
  apple green (475) and royal blue (495)
- 3D cutting sheet (429)
- Sulky embroidery thread: red and purple
- Red adhesive stones

Carefully read the instructions given in Techniques.

Card 1

Make a dark green double card (13.5 x 13.5 cm). Draw four corner pieces which are two squares high and two squares wide on apple green paper. Punch the two outer squares and cut the corner pieces out leaving a border. Stick the four corner pieces on cream paper and cut them out. Next, stick them on red paper and cut them out leaving a border. Emboss and embroider four patterns in cream card.
Cut the patterns out and stick them on the corner pieces. Stick all the layers on the card with the 3D picture in the middle. To decorate the card, add the inlays of the matching sticker and stick adhesive stones and sticker dots in the middle of the embroidered and punched patterns.

Card 2

Make a violet double card (10.5 x 14.8 cm). Stick three mosaic stickers alternately on apple green paper (2.2 cm wide and six squares long). Stick the inlays of those stickers on three cream squares (2.2 x 2.2 cm) and stick them on the three empty squares. Next, stick the strip on violet and cream paper and cut each layer out leaving a border. Stick the 3D picture on violet, cream and apple green paper and cut each layer out leaving a border. Finally, stick red adhesive stones on the stickers.

Card 3

Make a royal blue double card (13.5 x 13.5 cm). Punch four patterns in cream paper and cut them out. Stick the matching mosaic stickers on old red paper (2.2 x 2.2 cm). Stick the 3D picture on violet and cream paper and cut each layer out leaving a border. Cut an apple green square (12.5 x 12.5 cm) and stick the following items on this: the picture in the middle; the decorative sticker right on the frame, the punched squares in the corners and the old red squares in the middle between these. Decorate the card with adhesive stones.

IT'S AUTUMN 9

Card 4

Make a cream double card (10.5 x 14.8 cm). Stick the picture on dark green paper and cut it out leaving a border. Next, stick it on the left-hand side of the card together with a border sticker.

Draw one corner piece which is six squares high and three squares wide on apple green paper. Punch the patterns in every other square. Next, place the strip on a light box and prick the embroidery pattern. Cut the embroidered pattern out leaving a border. Stick four matching mosaic stickers on old red paper of the same size and stick these on the empty squares of the apple green strip as shown in the photograph.

stencil 2859

stencil 2860

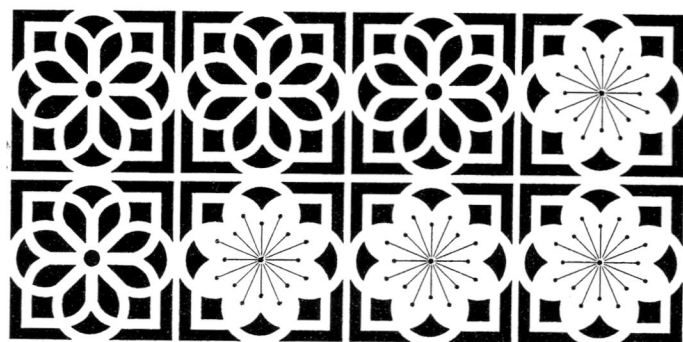

Spring is in the air

What you need
- ❏ *CQ embossing/embroidery stencils: 2859 and 2860*
- ❏ *Mosaic punches: 2859 and 2860*
- ❏ *CQ mosaic stickers: 2806 and 2812*
- ❏ *cArt-us card: aqua marine (427) and light blue (391)*
- ❏ *cArt-us punch paper:*
  aqua marine (427) and golden yellow (247)
- ❏ *Sulky embroidery thread: dark blue and gold*
- ❏ *Block 3D cutting sheet*
- ❏ *Adhesive stones: amber and dark blue*

Card 1
Make an aqua marine double card (13.5 x 13.5 cm) and stick a Picture Punch square on it. Punch and embroider four blue squares. Cut out the square in the middle of the card and stick the picture inside the card behind the opening. Use 3D glue to add extra flowers. Decorate the card with adhesive stones.

Card 2
Make a light blue double card (10.5 x 14.8 cm). Emboss a pattern in the top left-hand and bottom right-hand corners and embroider the patterns. Draw four corner pieces which are two squares high and two squares wide on aqua marine paper. Punch two patterns and cut the paper as shown in the photograph. Stick yellow paper behind them. Stick two pictures on aqua marine paper and cut them out leaving a border. Stick everything on the card and stick border stickers around the pictures. Decorate the card with adhesive stones.

Card 3
Make a light blue double card (14 x 14 cm) and stick three squares on it: golden yellow (12.5 x 12.5 cm), aqua marine (12 x 12 cm) and light blue (9 x 9 cm). Add some border stickers. Stick four mosaic stickers on golden yellow paper of the same size and use 3D glue to stick them on the card. Stick the picture in the middle of the card and use 3D glue to stick a 1.7 cm wide frame (6 x 6 cm) around it. Stick a flower frame on top. Use 3D glue to add some extra yellow squares. Decorate the card with adhesive stones.

Card 4
Make a light blue double card (10.5 x 14.8 cm) and two 1 cm wide golden yellow frames (5 x 5 cm). Add some border stickers and some adhesive stones. Cut the middle out of the frames and stick the pictures inside the card behind the openings. Stick three mosaic stickers on aqua marine paper of the same size and stick them, together with their inlays, on a light blue strip of paper (2.2 cm wide and six squares high) and stick the strip on a piece of golden yellow paper which is slightly larger.

SPRING IS IN THE AIR

LET THE SUN SHINE

Let the sun shine

What you need
- CQ embossing/embroidery stencils: 2859 and 2860
- Mosaic punch (2860)
- Gold CQ mosaic stickers: 2801, 2803, 2809 and 2811
- cArt-us card: aqua marine (427), dark green (309), golden yellow (247) and ochre (575)
- cArt-us punch paper: dark green (309)
- Sulky embroidery thread: dark blue and dark green
- Cutting sheet: IT 408
- Adhesive stones: amber

Card 1
Make an ochre double card (13.5 x 13.5 cm) and stick a dark green square (13 x 13 cm) on it. Cut four 2.2 cm wide strips of golden yellow paper: two which are five squares long and two which are three squares long. Emboss and embroider the patterns as shown in the photograph. Stick eight mosaic stickers on dark green paper of the same size and stick these on the empty squares. Stick the strips on aqua marine paper and cut them out leaving a border. Decorate the card with border stickers and adhesive stones.

Card 2
Make an ochre card (10.5 x 14.8 cm) and stick an aqua marine rectangle (10 x 14.8 cm) on it. Stick decorative stickers along the sides. Draw two strips which are three squares long on dark green paper. Punch the patterns in every other square and cut the strips out leaving a border. Stick the mosaic stickers between the punched patterns. Stick golden yellow paper under the strips. Prick and embroider the patterns. Stick both strips, together with the 3D picture, on an ochre rectangle (7 x 13.5 cm).

Card 3
Make an aqua marine double card (10.5 x 14.8 cm). Cut a golden yellow strip (2.2 x 11 cm). Stick two mosaic stickers on aqua marine paper of the same size and stick them on the strip alternately with the matching inlays of the stickers. Stick the strip on aqua marine paper, ochre paper, dark green paper and then yellow paper and cut each layer out leaving a border. Decorate the card with a 3D picture and adhesive stones.

Card 4
Make an aqua marine double card (10.5 x 14.8 cm). Make an ochre rectangle which is 0.5 cm smaller than the card and a dark green rectangle which 1 cm smaller than the card. Make four corner pieces which are two squares high and two squares wide. Stick eight mosaic stickers on aqua marine paper of the same size and then stick them, together with the matching inlays of the stickers, on the corner pieces. Decorate the card with a 3D picture and adhesive stones.

Pets in the Christmas spirit

What you need
- CQ embossing/embroidery stencils:
  2860, 2862, 2863 and 2864
- Mosaic punches:
  2860, 2862, 2863 and 2864
- Gold star stickers
- cArt-us card:
  green (367), mint (331) and old red (517)
- cArt-us punch paper: old red (517)
- Adhesive stones: dark green and red
- Sulky embroidery thread: green and red
- Cutting sheet:
  Picturel Pets in the Christmas spirit

Decorate the cards with sticker dots and adhesive stones.

Card 1
Make a green double card (14 x 14 cm) and an old red square (13.5 x 13.5 cm). Draw four corner pieces which are two squares high and two squares wide on mint green card. It is a good idea to use a punch aid for this. Punch the middle square and emboss the other squares. Embroider the patterns. Cut out the corner pieces, stick them on the old red square and punch a pattern between the corner pieces (see the photograph). Stick the 3D picture on a green square (7 x 7 cm). Stick all the layers on the card.

Card 2
Make an old red double card (10.5 x 14.8 cm) and stick a green rectangle (10 x 14.3 cm) on it. Draw a strip which is five squares long on mint green card. Alternately emboss and punch the patterns. Embroider all the patterns. Cut the strip out leaving a border, stick it on red card and cut it out leaving a border. Stick the strip and the 3D picture on the card.

Card 3
Make a green double card (13.5 x 13.5 cm) and stick two squares on it: old red (10 x 14.3 cm) and mint green (12.5 x 12.5 cm). Make a 3 cm wide mint green frame (12.5 x 12.5 cm). Draw a frame on it which is five squares high and five squares wide. Alternately punch and emboss the patterns on the frame. Prick and embroider the patterns in the embossed squares. Stick the frame and the 3D picture on the card.

Card 4
Make an old red double card (10.5 x 14.8 cm) and stick a green rectangle (10 x 14.3 cm) on it. Draw a corner piece which is four squares high and two squares wide on mint green card. Punch and emboss the squares. Cut the corner piece out leaving a border and stick it on old red card of the same size. Prick and embroider the patterns in all the squares. Stick the corner piece and the 3D picture on the card.

PETS IN THE CHRISTMAS SPIRIT

SNOWDROPS IN THE SNOW 17

Snowdrops in the snow

What you need
- ❑ Mosaic punches: 2860, 2863 and 2864
- ❑ Gold CQ mosaic stickers: 2803 and 2807
- ❑ cArt-us card: cream (241)
- ❑ Canson Mi-Teintes card: apple green (475)
- ❑ cArt-us punch paper: dark green (309)
- ❑ Sulky embroidery thread: gold
- ❑ Cutting sheet: Marjoleine Snowdrops
- ❑ Adhesive stones: green

Card 1
Make an apple green double card (13.5 x 13.5 cm) and stick two squares on it: cream (12.5 x 12.5 cm) and dark green (12 x 12 cm). Draw a frame which is five squares high and five squares wide on cream card. Emboss and embroider every other square. Stick the matching mosaic stickers between the embossed and embroidered squares (stick them on apple green paper first and cut them out). Cut out the middle of the frame through all the layers of card. Stick a dark green square (7 x 7 cm) inside the card behind the opening. Stick four pictures on this and five inlays of the matching mosaic sticker. Decorate the card with adhesive stones.

Card 2
Make an apple green card (10.5 x 14.8 cm). Cut out three pictures and stick them on cream paper (3.5 x 3.5 cm) and cut them out leaving a border. Stick the top and the bottom pictures on the card. Stick a 2 mm wide frame (3.5 x 3.5 cm) between them and cut out the middle. Stick the third picture inside the card behind the opening. Draw a strip which is six squares

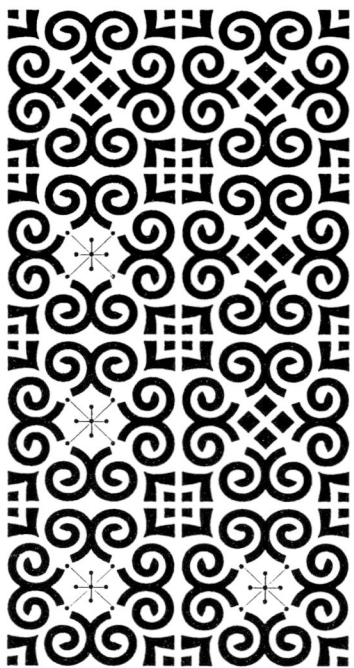

stencil 2861

long on dark green paper. Punch every other square and cut the strip out leaving a border. Stick it on cream paper (4 x 14.8 cm). Prick and embroider the patterns in the punched squares. Stick three matching mosaic stickers on apple green paper of the same size and stick these on the empty squares. Decorate the card with adhesive stones.

Card 3

Make a cream card (13.5 x 13.5 cm) and stick two squares on it: apple green (11.5 x 11.5 cm) and dark green (11 x 11 cm). Punch four dark green squares and cut out four pictures. Stick them 0.5 cm from the edge of a piece of cream paper (10 x 10 cm) as shown in the photograph. Prick and embroider the punched squares. Cut a square (3 x 3 cm) out of the middle of the card through all the layers and stick the same picture behind the opening. Decorate the card with adhesive stones.

Card 4

Make a cream double card (10.5 x 14.8 cm) and stick an apple green rectangle (9.5 x 13.8 cm) on it. Stick the picture in the middle and add some border stickers. Cut away the background of the picture through all the layers of card. Stick the same picture inside the card. Punch four dark green squares and stick them on cream paper of the same size. Prick and embroider the patterns. Stick the squares on the card and decorate them with adhesive stones.

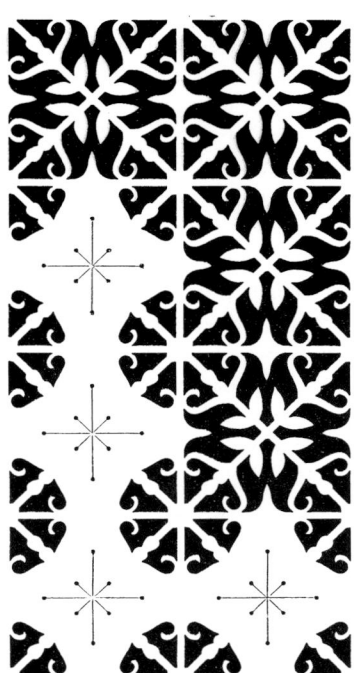

stencil 2862

The height of the summer

What you need
- ❏ CQ embossing/embroidery stencils:
  2860, 2861, 2863 and 2864
- ❏ Mosaic punch (2860)
- ❏ Gold CQ mosaic stickers: 2803, 2805, 2809 and 2811
- ❏ cArt-us card: aqua marine (427),
  dark blue (417) and spring green (305)
- ❏ cArt-us punch paper:
  dark blue (417), green (367) and spring green (305)
- ❏ Canson Mi-Teintes punch paper: royal blue (495)
- ❏ Sulky embroidery thread:
  dark blue and gold
- ❏ Cutting sheet: IT 407

Card 1
Make an aqua marine double card (11 x 14 cm). Draw four corner pieces which are two squares high and two squares wide on spring green card. Emboss and embroider the square in the corner. Stick eight matching mosaic stickers on dark blue paper of the same size. Stick these squares on the corner pieces. Stick the corner pieces on green paper and cut them out leaving a border. Decorate the card with a 3D picture and sticker dots.

Card 2
Make a dark blue double card (10.5 x 14.8 cm). Draw a corner piece which is six squares high and four squares wide on spring green card. Emboss and embroider four squares. Stick the mosaic stickers on royal blue paper of the same size and stick these on the empty squares. Stick the corner piece on green paper and cut it out leaving a border. Stick the picture on spring green paper and cut it out leaving a border.

Card 3
Make a spring green card (13.5 x 13.5 cm) and stick a green square (12.5 x 12.5 cm) on it. Draw a frame which is five squares high and five squares wide on dark blue paper (12 x 12 cm). Punch the squares as shown in the photograph. Stick spring green paper (11.5 x 11.5 cm) behind it and prick and embroider the patterns. Stick eight matching mosaic stickers on royal blue paper of the same size and stick these on the empty squares. Stick the 3D picture in the middle.

Card 4
Make a spring green double card (10.5 x 14.8 cm). Stick three mosaic stickers on spring green paper of the same size. Cut a dark blue strip (14.8 x 2.2 cm) and alternately stick the mosaic stickers and the inlays of the stickers on it. Stick the strip on green paper and cut it out leaving a border. Stick the 3D picture on aqua marine paper and cut it out leaving a 0.5 cm wide border.

THE HEIGHT OF THE SUMMER

It's Christmas

What you need
- ❏ *CQ embossing/embroidery stencils:*
  2859, 2860, 2861 and 2863
- ❏ *Mosaic punches: 2859, 2860 and 2863*
- ❏ *Gold CQ mosaic stickers: 2801, 2803, 2805 and 2809*
- ❏ *Canson Mi-Teintes card:*
  apple green (475) and light blue (490)
- ❏ *cArt-us punch paper: dark red and elephant skin*
- ❏ *Sulky embroidery thread: gold*
- ❏ *Cutting sheets: 3D 432 and 3D 435*
- ❏ *Adhesive stones: amber*

Carefully read the instructions given in Techniques.

Card 1
Make an apple green double card (10.5 x 14.8 cm) and stick a piece of elephant skin paper of the same size on it. Stick the 3D picture on light blue paper and cut it out leaving a border. Stick this on the right-hand side of the card and stick border stickers on both sides. Draw a strip which is six squares long on dark red paper. Punch every other square. Cut the strip out leaving a border. Stick the strip on elephant skin paper and cut it out. Prick and embroider the patterns. Stick the matching inlays of the stickers on the empty squares. Stick the strip on light blue and apple green paper and cut each layer out leaving a border. Add some adhesive stones.

Card 2
Make an apple green card (13.5 x 13.5 cm) and add some border stickers as shown in the photograph. Draw four squares on dark red paper and punch them. Cut them out leaving a border and stick the squares on elephant skin paper of the same size. Prick and embroider the patterns. Stick the picture on light blue paper and elephant skin paper and cut each layer out leaving a border. Cut out the pictures in the bottom left-hand corner and the top right-hand corner of the card and stick a complete picture inside the card behind the openings. Make the pictures which are visible when the card is closed 3D. Stick everything on the card and decorate the corners with adhesive stones.

Card 3
Make a light blue double card (13.5 x 13.5 cm). Draw four corner pieces which are two squares high and two squares wide on dark red paper. Punch two squares of each corner piece and cut the corner pieces out leaving a border. Stick matching mosaic stickers on the squares in the corners. Stick elephant skin paper behind the corner pieces and cut them out. Prick and embroider the patterns. Stick the corner pieces on the card. Stick the picture on apple green paper and cut it out leaving a border. Cut away the beige background from the 3D picture through all

the layers of card and stick the same picture inside the card behind the opening. Add some border stickers.

Card 4

Make a light blue card (10.5 x 14.8 cm). Stick the 3D picture on dark red and apple green paper and cut each layer out leaving a border. Stick the picture in the bottom right-hand corner of the card and cut away the beige background. Stick the same picture inside the card and stick some adhesive stones on the background of this picture. Draw a corner piece which is five squares high and three squares wide on dark red paper. Stick the mosaic stickers and the matching inlays of the stickers on alternate squares. Stick the corner piece on apple green paper and cut it out leaving a border. Make the picture 3D and add some adhesive stones.

stencil 2864

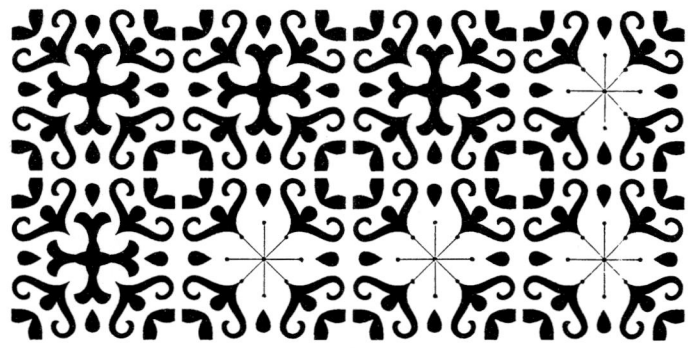

stencil 2863

24 IT'S CHRISTMAS

SPARKLING CANDLES

Sparkling candles

What you need
- ❏ CQ embossing/embroidery stencils: 2859, 2860, 2862 and 2863
- ❏ Mosaic punch (2860)
- ❏ Gold CQ mosaic stickers: 2801, 2803, 2807 and 2809
- ❏ Gold star stickers
- ❏ cArt-us card: terracotta (549) and ochre (575)
- ❏ cArt-us punch paper: cream (211) and dark green (309)
- ❏ Romak separating sheets (130 g): light blue satin finish rectangle (3416) and light blue satin finish square (3421)
- ❏ Sulky embroidery thread: copper
- ❏ 3D cutting sheet (433)
- ❏ Adhesive stones: dark green
- ❏ Gold glitter glue (Duncan)

Carefully read the instructions given in Techniques. Add a small amount of glitter glue to the 3D pictures and allow it to dry.

Card 1

Make an ochre double card (13.5 x 13.5 cm) and stick a terracotta square (13 x 13 cm) on it. Draw two strips which are five squares long on a light blue separating sheet and emboss two squares. Embroider the squares according to the patterns and stick matching mosaic stickers on the empty squares. Cut the strips out. Stick them both on dark green paper and cut them out leaving a border. Stick the strips and the 3D picture on the card. Add some adhesive stones and sticker dots.

Card 2

Cut 3.2 cm off the right-hand side of an ochre double card (14.8 x 10.5 cm). Draw a strip which is six squares long on a light blue separating sheet. Emboss the desired figure in three alternate squares and embroider the patterns. Stick matching mosaic stickers on the empty squares and cut the strip out. Stick the strip on dark green and terracotta paper and cut each layer out leaving a border. Stick the strip inside the card 0.5 cm from the right-hand side and the bottom of the card. Stick the 3D picture on a light blue separating sheet (13.7 x 5.7 cm) and then on dark green and terracotta paper. Cut each layer out leaving a border. Stick the picture on the front of the card and add some adhesive stones and sticker dots.

Card 3

Make a terracotta double card (13.5 x 13.5 cm) and stick two squares on it: dark green (12.5 x 12.5 cm) and ochre (11 x 11 cm). Stick the 3D picture on a light blue separating sheet (9.4 x 9.4 cm). Stick four mosaic stickers on cream paper of the same size and then on green squares which are slightly larger. Prick holes according to the pattern and then embroider a pattern. Stick everything on the card as shown in the photograph and add some sticker dots.

punch 2859

Card 4

Make a terracotta double card (10.5 x 14.8 cm) and stick an ochre rectangle (10.3 x 14.6 cm) on it. Draw a corner piece which is six squares high and four squares wide on dark green card. Punch alternate squares. Cut the corner piece out leaving a border and stick it on the left-hand side of a piece of satin finish paper (9.5 x 13.8 cm). Prick and embroider the patterns in the punched squares. Stick matching stickers on the empty squares. Decorate the card with sticker dots and adhesive stones.

punch 2860

punch 2861

Playful butterflies

What you need
- CQ embossing/embroidery stencils: 2860 and 2864
- Mosaic punches: 2860 and 2864
- Gold CQ mosaic stickers: 2805, 2807 and 2811
- cArt-us card: aqua marine (427), cornflower blue (393), light blue (391) and lilac (453)
- cArt-us punch paper: aqua blue (427)
- Sulky embroidery thread: gold and dark blue
- Cutting sheet: Picturel Butterflies
- Adhesive stones: purple

Card 1
Make a light blue double card (13.5 x 13.5 cm). Draw corner pieces which are two squares high and two squares wide on aqua marine paper. Punch the squares. Stick the corner pieces on cornflower blue paper and cut them out leaving a border. Embroider the patterns. Stick matching mosaic stickers on lilac paper of the same size. Stick the 3D picture on an aqua marine square (6.5 x 6.5 cm).

Card 2
Make a lilac double card (10.5 x 14.8 cm). Stick the 3D picture on light blue paper (5 x 13.5 cm) and then on aqua marine paper which is slightly larger. Stick three mosaic stickers on aqua marine paper of the same size and then stick them on a light blue strip (13.2 cm) alternating with the matching inlays of the stickers. Stick the strip on cornflower blue paper and cut it out leaving a border. Decorate the card as shown in the photograph.

Card 3
Make a light blue double card (10.5 x 14.8 cm). Stick the picture on an aqua marine strip (3 x 13 cm) and then on cornflower blue paper (6 x 13 cm). Stick the strip on lilac paper and cut it out leaving a border. Stick the strip on the card and add some border stickers. Make the strip on the left-hand side as described for card 2. Stick the strip on cornflower blue and aqua marine paper and cut each layer out leaving a border.

Card 4
Make a cornflower blue double card (13.5 x 13.5 cm). Stick the 3D picture on a light blue piece of paper (7 x 7 cm). Stick this on aqua marine paper and cut it out leaving a border. Stick the square on the card and add some border stickers. Cut three aqua marine strips of paper (7 x 2.2 cm). Punch the ends and stick the strips on light blue paper of the same size. Emboss four figures in the lilac card, embroider the patterns and stick the squares on the strips.

PLAYFUL BUTTERFLIES 29

Large and small stickers

What you need
- Mosaic punch (2860)
- Gold CQ mosaic stickers: 2803, 2805, 2809 and 2811
- cArt-us card: dark blue (417), dark green (309), light blue (391) and terracotta (549)
- cArt-us punch paper: aqua marine (427), dark blue (417), green (367), cornflower blue (393), lavender (487), spring green (305), mint (331), pink (481), violet (425) and soft pink (485)
- Adhesive stones: amber and green

All the cards measure 13.5 x 13.5 cm.
Stick paper of a different colour behind the middle of the large stickers. If the paper is visible behind the wrong openings, cut it off before adding the next colour.

Card 1
Make a light blue double card and stick two squares on it: cornflower blue (12 x 12 cm) and light blue (11.2 x 11.2 cm). Add some border stickers. Draw a frame which is five blocks high and five blocks wide on a 2.8 cm wide dark blue frame (11.5 x 11.5 cm). Punch alternate squares. Stick eight matching mosaic stickers on cornflower blue paper of the same size and stick these on the empty squares. Stick cornflower blue paper behind the middle of the large sticker, light blue paper behind the edge of the figure and dark blue paper behind the straight edges of the square. Stick the sticker on the card as shown in the photograph and add some corner stickers. Decorate the card with adhesive stones.

Card 2
Make a dark blue double card. Draw corner pieces which are four squares high and four squares wide on lilac paper. Stick six mosaic stickers on dark blue paper of the same size. Stick the stickers and the matching inlays of the stickers alternately on the card. Stick the strips on violet and lavender paper

and cut each layer out leaving a border. Take two large stickers and stick the following colours behind them: lavender in the middle, lilac behind the petals, violet behind the triangles and dark blue behind the corners. Next, stick each sticker on lavender, dark blue and then lilac paper and cut each layer out leaving a border. Stick one sticker in the middle of the card. Cut the front of the card diagonally through the middle and around the dark blue border of the large sticker. Stick the second sticker inside the card, exactly under the sticker on the front of the card, so that the coloured borders are aligned. Stick one corner piece on the front of the card and one inside the card.

Card 3

Make a dark green double card and stick two squares on it: mint green (11 x 11 cm) and spring green (11.5 x 11.5 cm). Stick nine mosaic stickers on dark green squares of the same size. Stick them and the matching inlays of the stickers alternately around the edge of the card. Stick paper of different colours behind the large sticker: spring green in the middle and behind the triangles, green behind the flower and the small corners. Stick the sticker on mint green and spring green paper and cut each layer out leaving a border. Decorate the card with border stickers and some adhesive stones.

Card 4

This card is made in the same way as card 2, except that different colours are used. Terracotta card is used for the double card. The corner pieces are pink and stuck on soft pink and pink paper. The mosaic stickers are stuck on terracotta paper. The same colour combination is used behind the large stickers. Stick a purple adhesive stone in the middle and add some border stickers.

punch 2862   *punch 2864*

punch 2863

Shopkeepers can order the materials used from Kars & Co B.V. in Ochten, the Netherlands.

32 LARGE AND SMALL STICKERS